COLLINS GEM
CATS

a mine of information

D1348345

COLLINS GEM
classic
FILMS

COLLINS GEM
HORSES
& PONIES

a mine of information

COLLINS GEM
INSECTS

a mine of information

COLLINS GEM
KINGS &
QUEENS

a mine of information

COLLINS GEM
MUSHROOMS
& TOADSTOOLS

a mine of information

COLLINS GEM
SNAKES

a mine of information

COLLINS GEM
SPIDERS

a mine of information

COLLINS GEM
STRESS
Survival Guide

a mine of information

COLLINS GEM
TAROT

a mine of information

COLLINS GEM
WINE
Guide

a mine of information

COLLINS GEM
WORLD
atlas

a mine of information

COLLINS GEM
YOGA

a mine of information

COLLINS GEM
ZODIAC
Types

a mine of information

Contents

INTRODUCTION

THERE is something special about whales, dolphins and porpoises. They are still shrouded in mystery, yet the little we do know about them is both astonishing and awe-inspiring. They include the largest animal on Earth, the deepest-diving mammal, the mammal with the longest known migration, species that are capable of emitting the loudest sounds in nature, and many other extraordinary creatures. They also include some of the world's most critically endangered species.

Humpback whale, Dominican Republic

Watching them in the wild is probably the ultimate wildlife experience. Who could ever forget the sight of a 50 tonne southern right whale launching itself high into the air, or of a sperm whale diving into the cold, dark depths hundreds or even thousands of metres below the surface? Who could fail to be intrigued by Longman's beaked whale, which is known only from two weathered skulls, or remain untouched by the plight of the last few surviving Yangtze river dolphins?

It is not surprising that more than five million people join organised whale and dolphin watching trips, in at least 65 different countries and independent territories around the world, every year.

The aim of this book is to introduce the world of whales, dolphins and porpoises and to summarise our current knowledge about them. It includes information on their evolution, biology and natural history, describes how they are studied, the threats they face, and some of the efforts to protect the ones most in trouble. It also explains how, where and when to watch them around the world, and includes a directory of all 81 recognised species.

Striped dolphin, Gibraltar

ALL ABOUT WHALES, DOLPHINS & PORPOISES

Natural History
Evolution

WHALES, dolphins and porpoises are believed to have evolved from a group of furry land mammals called the mesonychids (illustrated right). These strange creatures looked rather like wolves but had hooves like cows and deer. They lived around the ancient Tethys Sea, an area that is now the Mediterranean Sea and part of the Asian sub-continent, about 60 million years ago.

The mesonychids probably spent their lives foraging for fish and other aquatic animals in coastal swamps and estuaries. As they spent more and more time in the water their bodies began to change. They became more streamlined and developed powerful, flattened tails; their forelimbs gradually turned into paddles and their hindlimbs wasted away; they developed insulating layers of fat and their body hair began to disappear; and, to help them to breathe at the water's surface, their nostrils started to move towards the top of their heads to become blowholes.

The first real whale-like animals, or archaeocetes, appeared about 10 million years later, and spread rapidly throughout the oceans of the world – their fossilised remains have been found as far afield as Britain, Canada, Australia and even Antarctica.

They were probably very similar to modern whales, dolphins and porpoises, although they were less well adapted to life in the sea. They may even have clambered back onto land to breed, just like modern seals.

The last of the archaeocetes probably died out about 30 million years ago and, by this time, representatives of modern whales, dolphins and porpoises were fairly common and widespread. None were exactly the same as the species alive today, but they were unmistakably similar in appearance and in their way of life. By about five million years ago most, if not all, modern families of whales, dolphins and porpoises had become firmly established.

Diversity

THE sheer diversity of whales, dolphins and porpoises tends to surprise many people. There are no fewer than 81 recognised species altogether and, as research progresses, new discoveries continue to be made. The Peruvian or lesser beaked whale, for example, was described in the scientific literature in 1991, and is yet to be seen alive. Yet another beaked whale, this time from a group of islands off the coast of Chile, was formally named Bahamonde's beaked whale as recently as 1996.

Meanwhile, the latest genetic research is revealing that some animals previously thought to be single species should actually be split. In 1995, for example, the common dolphin was officially

Common dolphin, California, USA

Fin whale, Mexico

separated into two distinct species, the short-beaked common dolphin and the long-beaked common dolphin.

While all these animals share many characteristics, there is no 'typical' whale, dolphin or porpoise. They range from tiny dolphins and porpoises just over 1 m long, to whales that are known to reach lengths of more than 30 m. The heaviest species is no less than 3,000 times heavier than the lightest. Some are long and slender, others short and stocky. Some have huge dorsal fins, others have no fins at all. Many are brightly-coloured or striking in black and white, others are rather drab.

Some live in freezing cold waters near the poles, others prefer the warmer waters of the tropics. Many live in the middle of the deepest oceans, others prefer to be much closer to shore, while a few even live hundreds of kilometres inland in rivers such as the Yangtze, the Ganges and the Amazon.

Is it a whale, a dolphin or a porpoise?

WHALES, dolphins and porpoises are known collectively as cetaceans. Interestingly, there is no real scientific basis for splitting cetaceans into these three groups. Broadly speaking, the word 'whale' is used to describe the largest animals, 'dolphin' to describe the medium-sized ones, and 'porpoise' to describe the smallest. But some whales are smaller than the largest dolphins, and some dolphins are smaller than the largest porpoises.

There are many more confusing names and terms, as well. The rightwhale dolphins, for example, were named after right whales but are actually dolphins. At the same time, many are known by umpteen different names in at least as many different languages. Thus the northern giant bottlenose whale, North Pacific bottlenose whale, giant four-toothed whale, northern four-toothed whale and

Bottlenose dolphin, Australia

Humpback whale, New England, USA

Baird's beaked whale are all the same species.

Even more confusing are six members of the dolphin family which have the word 'whale' in their names: killer whale, pygmy killer whale, false killer whale, melon-headed whale, long-finned pilot whale and short-finned pilot whale. These are often classified together in a group known as the 'blackfish', which is also rather strange since not all of them are black and, of course, none are fish.

Scientists prefer to split modern cetaceans into just two distinct groups: the toothed whales, or Odontocetes, and the baleen whales, or Mysticetes. As their name suggests, the toothed whales possess teeth; this group of 70 species includes all the beaked whales, sperm whales, blackfish, oceanic dolphins, river dolphins and porpoises. The baleen whales make up the remaining 11 species and, instead of teeth, have hundreds of strange-looking baleen plates hanging down from their upper jaws; they include most of the larger and more popular whales, for example the blue, humpback, grey and right whales.

Inside and out

Whales, dolphins and porpoises are so
streamlined, and so well adapted to life
underwater, that they look rather like sharks and
other large fish. They even have similar dorsal fins,
flippers and powerful tails. But appearances can be
deceptive. The similarities between them are simply
the result of two unrelated groups of animals
adapting in similar ways to identical living
conditions. On closer inspection, there are actually
more differences between them than there are
similarities.

Fish are cold-blooded, use their gills to extract all
the oxygen they need directly from the water, and
normally lay eggs or give birth to young that can
feed themselves. In contrast, whales, dolphins and
porpoises are mammals, like us, and so are warm-
blooded, breathe air with lungs, and give birth to
young that feed on their mother's milk for the first
weeks or months of life.

One of the most striking features of any cetacean
is the thick layer of fat under the skin, known as
blubber, which they have instead of hair or fur. This
helps them to keep warm in water, which sucks heat
out of a mammal up to twenty-five times faster than
air.

A detailed look inside their bodies, as shown in
these diagrams, reveals many other interesting
features and adaptations for their underwater life.

ANATOMY OF A CETACEAN

elongated skull bones (upper jaw, or rostrum, and lower jaw, or mandible, are unusually long)

some or all of neck vertebrae fused as an adaptation for swimming at high speed

no bony support for dorsal fin (made of a tough, fibrous material)

flexible backbone extends down through centre of tail stock to beginning of flukes

no bony support for flukes (made of same tough, fibrous material as dorsal fin)

two small pieces of bone are all that remain of the hind limbs and pelvis

front limbs have turned into flippers, or pectoral fins, yet the original structure of the arm, hand and finger bones is still visible

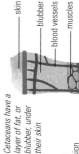

skin

blubber

blood vessels

muscles

Cetaceans have a layer of fat, or blubber, under their skin

thin layer of skin

backbone

muscle in the tail provides powerful means of propulsion

thick layer of blubber

Diving and swimming

THE fastest speed ever achieved by a human swimmer is an incredible 8.64 km/h. Equally impressive, the deepest anyone has ever dived while holding their breath is 157 m. But these superhuman feats barely register on the scale of swimming and diving records achieved by whales, dolphins and porpoises. Killer whales, Dall's porpoises and several other species have been clocked at speeds of up to 55 km/h, while sperm whales (and, possibly, some beaked whales) can dive to depths of at least 2,000 m and have been known to stay underwater for more than two hours at a time.

All cetaceans breathe air and, consequently, have to hold their breath whenever they disappear underwater. Their lungs are relatively small, but they are able to extract much more oxygen from the air than human lungs and then use it far more efficiently.

Human sub-aqua divers can suffer from a potentially fatal condition known as decompression sickness, or the bends. It is caused by nitrogen bubbling out of the blood, either when the divers stay down for too long or when they rise to the surface too quickly. These bubbles then lodge in joints and cause severe pain, or in vital blood vessels and cause paralysis or even death. Whales, dolphins and porpoises do not suffer from the bends. Since they are holding their breath when they dive, they are not continually breathing in more nitrogen.

Short-finned pilot whales, Canary Islands

Also, their lungs collapse under pressure, trapping the air in the thick-walled windpipe and nasal passages, where nitrogen cannot be absorbed into the blood.

On deep dives, human sub-aqua divers can suffer from another dangerous condition, called nitrogen narcosis. They start losing control over what they are doing, as if they are drunk. Although nitrogen narcosis is not dangerous in itself, it makes accidents far more likely. Whales, dolphins and porpoises do not suffer from nitrogen narcosis because it is induced by breathing nitrogen under pressure (from a scuba tank) and they breathe it only at the surface.

Food and feeding

MOST whales, dolphins and porpoises feed on fish, squid or crustaceans, although some will take a wide variety of other prey as well.

Between them, they have an astonishing range of different hunting techniques. For example, killer whales in Patagonia beach themselves to catch sea lion pups; strap-toothed whales suck squid into their mouths so quickly they appear to have been attached to pieces of invisible elastic; belugas blast powerful jets of water to dislodge fish hiding in mud on the seabed; open-ocean dolphins work together to corral fish against the surface of the sea; and blue whales take huge quantities of seawater into their

Fin whale, Iceland

mouths, and then filter out as much as four tonnes of shrimp-like krill every day.

In turn, they themselves are preyed upon by large sharks and even by some of their own kind: killer whales, false killer whales and pygmy killer whales. The smaller species are most at risk, but no whale is too large for a determined pod of killer whales.

TEETH

As their name suggests, all toothed whales have teeth. But the number varies greatly from species to species and, in some female beaked whales, they do not actually erupt. Cetacean teeth come in a variety of shapes and sizes, but each species has just one design; in other words, they are not differentiated into incisors, canines, pre-molars and molars. Unlike other mammals, toothed whales do not have two sets of teeth, but retain their first set for life.

Bowhead   Fin   Minke

Baleen

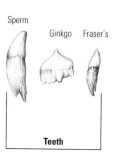

Sperm   Ginkgo   Fraser's

Teeth

BALEEN PLATES

Instead of teeth, most large whales have hundreds of strange-looking structures hanging down from their upper jaws. These are called baleen plates. They overlap one another, inside the mouth, to form bristly sieves for filtering small animals out of the seawater. Some 400–700 baleen plates is typical for most whales, but their number, size and shape varies greatly from species to species.

KRILL

Krill are small, shrimp-like crustaceans. Full of protein, and living in dense swarms, they make ideal food for large whales. There are at least 80 different species of krill, ranging in length from 8–60 mm, but perhaps the most important is the 5–6 cm Antarctic krill. This is the staple food of most baleen whales in the Antarctic, as well as of fish, squid, penguins and seals. The total population of krill in the Southern Ocean has been estimated at 600,000 billion, and they live in such enormous swarms that it is possible to track them by satellites in space. One particular swarm, tracked by US scientists off Antarctica in March 1981, was estimated to weigh an incredible 10 million tonnes.

Migration

MANY large baleen whales have little choice but to split their year into four distinctive parts. They spend a few months, in the summer, gorging themselves on schooling fish and krill in high-latitude, cold water feeding grounds; in the autumn they migrate to low-latitude, warm water breeding grounds; then they spend a few months, during the winter, mating and calving; and finally, in the spring, they migrate all the way back to their feeding grounds, and the annual cycle begins all over again.

The problem they face is that most of their food is in colder regions, towards the sub-Arctic and the Antarctic. In an ideal world, this is where they would live year-round. Unfortunately, though, the food is only present in large quantities during the summer and, even if they stayed for the winter to breed, their newborn calves probably could not survive the freezing cold temperatures. In other words, their preferred feeding and breeding grounds are thousands of kilometres apart.

In most cases, the details of their migrations are still a mystery. How do they know when to leave, and when to return? How do they find their way? Do they stop to rest or feed? Do they swim near the surface, or travel at depth? There are many unanswered questions.

Not all large baleen whales undertake these extensive migrations. Bryde's, minke and pygmy right whales are able to live in non-extreme temperatures year-round, while sei whales, and some humpbacks and greys, do not complete their journeys if they find adequate food supplies en route. Fin whales in Mexico's Sea of Cortez, and blue whales in the northern Indian Ocean, seem to be permanent residents, while bowhead whales simply move backwards and forwards in their high Arctic home, with the advancing and retreating ice.

Regular long-distance migrations are virtually unknown in toothed whales, with one major exception. While female and young sperm whales spend most of their lives in warm waters, many of the older males are believed to move to rich feeding grounds, in high-latitude cold waters, during the spring and summer.

Humpback whale, Ecuador

Reproduction and social life

THERE are almost as many different reproductive strategies and ways of living together as there are species of whales, dolphins and porpoises. But it is a difficult field of research, and we are only just beginning to learn about the private lives of some better-known species.

- The age of **sexual maturity** varies greatly from species to species. At one extreme, male sperm whales are not sexually mature until they are about 18–21 years old; even then, they often have to wait another few years before they are big and strong enough to gain access to receptive females. At the other extreme, female harbour porpoises reach sexual maturity at about three years old and begin to breed the following year.

  After reaching breeding age, the females of most species spend their entire adult lives either with a calf by their side or a foetus growing inside them – or both.

- **Courtship and mating** can be long and involved affairs, with leaping, games of chase, touching and caressing for several hours before the two animals join together, belly to belly, although the details vary greatly from one species to another.

  It has never been known for one male cetacean to mate exclusively with one female. In the sperm whale, beaked whales and some other species, one male mates with many females; but

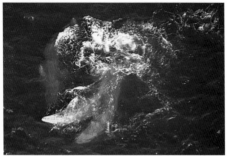

Mating group of grey whales, Mexico

most cetaceans are believed to be promiscuous:
each individual mates with numerous other
individuals of the opposite sex.

- The **gestation period** is unknown for many
  cetaceans, but seems to range from about 10
  months to as long as 17 months; there is a
  possible record of 18 months 28 days for one
  particular sperm whale. Surprisingly, it is not
  dependent on body size: in the blue whale, for
  example, it is roughly 11–12 months, whereas in
  the much smaller narwhal it is at least 14
  months.

- Few cetacean **births** have been witnessed in
  captivity, and even fewer in the wild, but we are
  gradually building up a reasonable picture of
  what happens.

Like most mammals, whales, dolphins and porpoises give birth to live young, although they normally have just one at a time. The calves are born underwater, near the surface where it is easier for them to catch their first breath, and their eyes are already open. They are able to swim, albeit a little awkwardly, almost as soon as they enter the water.

The calves are virtually identical to their parents, although their dorsal fins and tail flukes are more rubbery and they do not have baleen or teeth (which begin to erupt when they are a few weeks old). They are normally about a third of the length of their mothers; a newborn blue whale, for example, is an incredible 7 m long and weighs some 3 tonnes.

Bottlenose dolphin giving birth

- It is believed that the father plays no active role in **caring for the calf**, so it is the mother's responsibility alone. Suckling takes place underwater, and she literally squirts her rich, fat-laden milk into the young animal's mouth. The calf grows quickly. A young blue whale, for example, grows almost 4 cm and gains 90 kg every day – equivalent to the weight of average adult man.

  Weaning is usually gradual, with a period of overlap when the calf is drinking milk and eating solid food at the same time. It stays with its mother for weeks, months or even years afterwards, depending on the species. In general, toothed whales tend to have fewer young and look after them for a relatively long time, whereas baleen whales have more young and look after them for a relatively short time.

Sperm whale mother and calf, Mexico

- It is difficult to assess the ages of whales, dolphins and porpoises accurately and the maximum **life span** for most species is unknown. However, the limited information available suggests that the larger whales tend to have the longest life spans – possibly in excess of 100 years in the bowhead whale and some others. Smaller species, such as the harbour porpoise, may have an average life-expectancy of less than eight years.

  The two main natural causes of death are predation and disease. A variety of accidents and, of course, human-induced deaths also take their toll.

- Whales, dolphins and porpoises often have complex **social lives** and have adopted many different ways of living together. Some prefer to live alone, or in small groups, while others roam the seas in the company of hundreds or thousands of their contemporaries. Historically, there are even records of dolphin schools at least 100,000-strong.

  Some groups, such as orca pods, are fairly stable over periods of months or years. Others are incredibly fluid and their membership changes all the time, with individuals coming and going quite freely. Often, the membership of a group will vary according to specific requirements on a day-by-day or even hour-by-hour basis.

COMMONLY ASKED QUESTIONS
How intelligent are they?

ARE whales, dolphins and porpoises as intelligent as we would like to believe? They certainly *seem* to be intelligent: they have large brains, frequently live in complex societies, help one another in times of trouble, learn from experience, are often playful, and sometimes even seem to enjoy human company.

But, in truth, no-one really knows. Some people claim that they are no more intelligent than cats and dogs, while others go so far as to say that they may be our intellectual superiors.

There are two main reasons for this confusion. The first lies in defining what we mean by 'intelligent' and then taking meaningful measurements. Many definitions have been proposed over the years but, generally, intelligent animals are considered able to solve problems by grasping fundamental principles, and then making considered judgements, rather than trying to get things right by trial and error.

Obtaining accurate measurements of intelligence is another matter altogether. It is hard enough in humans, but it is even more challenging in other animals, which cannot talk or work with tools such as pens or computers.

The second reason is that any discussion of intelligence tends to be highly subjective. After all, we have only a human perspective, and can scarcely imagine what goes on inside another animal's mind.

The simple fact that whales, dolphins and porpoises have embarked on a completely different evolutionary path from our own makes any comparison almost impossible. Human intelligence suits our own way of life and, consequently, a large part of our brain deals with the use of hands to write, paint, sculpt, build or manipulate objects which exist outside our own bodies.

If we were to judge whales and dolphins on these terms, they would fare badly. But their intelligence suits a completely different way of life, and may concentrate instead on social skills, emotional self-control and other more spiritual and philosophical requirements.

Taking this into consideration, many people would argue that whales and dolphins are far more intelligent in their world than we are in ours.

Bottlenose dolphin and human friend, New Zealand

Why do they strand?

EVERY year, hundreds or even thousands of whales, dolphins and porpoises are found stranded on coastlines all over the world. They may be alive or dead, alone or in groups, and healthy or unwell. These strandings have probably been happening for thousands or even millions of years. But *why* they happen remains one of the great unsolved mysteries of the animal kingdom.

Some animals simply die at sea and are washed ashore with the tides and currents. But live strandings are far more mysterious. Theories put forward to explain their possible cause range from navigational problems as a result of changes in the Earth's magnetic field (quite possible) to mass suicide bids (highly unlikely). In reality, there may be different explanations in different cases, depending on the species, location and a variety of other factors.

Learning how to save stranded cetaceans with a model whale, Scotland

WHAT TO DO IF YOU FIND A STRANDED ANIMAL

Rescuing a stranded whale, dolphin or porpoise is extremely difficult. Well-intentioned, but misdirected, efforts can cause considerable stress to the animal and may even result in its death. It can also be quite dangerous to attempt a rescue, since even small cetaceans have been known to injure human helpers when they thrash around. These very basic guidelines are designed merely to make a stranded animal as comfortable as possible.

1 Call the local police immediately (for expert help); attempt a rescue yourself only if such expert help is unavailable.

2 Try to keep the animal upper side up, taking care not to trap either of the flippers under its body, and never pushing or pulling on the flippers, flukes, or head.

3 Keep the animal's skin moist and cool, with wet towels or water, but be careful not to cover the blowhole (or to let either water or sand enter the blowhole).

4 Erect a shelter to provide shade from the sun, but never apply suntan lotion to the animal's skin.

5 Keep onlookers and their dogs at a distance, make as little noise as possible, and do not touch the animal more than necessary.

6 Never, under any circumstances, attempt to destroy a stranded animal yourself.

How do they sleep?

THE way in which whales, dolphins and porpoises sleep has baffled and intrigued scientists for a very long time. Aristotle seemed particularly excited, centuries ago, when he noted that 'there are even people who have heard a dolphin snore'.

Over the years, of course, there have been some interesting theories. One was that they haul themselves out of the sea after dark and then spend the night curled up on shore in the company of seals and sea lions; no-one had actually seen them doing it, but the idea probably seemed quite logical at the time. Another theory was that they simply dive down to the seabed, make themselves comfortable, and lie there for the night.

In fact, the truth is even stranger than all this fiction. Unlike most other mammals, cetaceans never fall into a deep sleep, and they do not seem to have regular sleeping patterns linked to night and day. They do sleep, of course, though not in the way we might expect.

The reason is simple. Since our breathing is automatic, we can safely sleep and breathe at the same time. But cetaceans control their breathing consciously, so they have to be awake, and able to think, in order to take regular breaths. If they were to fall into a deep sleep, which is a naturally-occurring state of unconsciousness, they would drown.

Dusky dolphin, New Zealand

Instead of long periods of deep sleep, their solution is to swim along slowly, or lie just below the surface, and take short 'cat-naps'. They are believed to go into a semi-conscious state by switching off one half of the brain at a time. Then they swap sides to ensure that both halves are fully rested. While one side of the brain is asleep, the other remains awake to control the breathing and, of course, to look out for predators.

Should they be kept in captivity?

DURING the past century, more than 25 species of whales, dolphins and porpoises have been kept in captivity in zoos, marine parks and aquariums around the world. Thousands of individual animals have been captured in the wild, mainly to perform special shows for the fee-paying public. They are trained to jump through hoops, balance balls on their heads, 'kiss' their trainers, perform somersaults and synchronised leaps, and to do many other tricks.

Their owners argue that the animals 'enjoy' the shows, and are fortunate to be safe from predators, pollution and other threats in the wild. They point out that, as the undisputed stars of zoos and marine parks, they are worth a great deal of money and, directly or indirectly, provide thousands of people with secure jobs. They also claim that captive animals encourage members of the public to take an interest in the conservation of their wild relatives.

Some facilities are obviously much better than others, and whales and dolphins are kept in a bewildering range of establishments, from dirty hotel pools to professional marine parks with large,

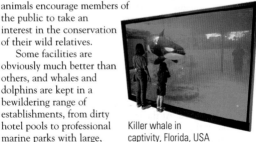

Killer whale in captivity, Florida, USA

Bottlenose dolphin in captivity, The Bahamas

coastal enclosures that are filled naturally with seawater and flushed with every new tide. Many of the animals are treated abominably, while a lucky few receive the best care that money can buy.

But most conservation and animal welfare groups are strongly opposed to keeping whales, dolphins or porpoises in captivity of any kind. Taken from the wild, and separated from their well-structured family groups, the animals are often forced to live alone or with unfamiliar species. Many of them are kept in small and featureless concrete tanks, where they can no longer hunt or hear the sounds of the sea, and may even be deprived of natural sunlight. They have to eat dead fish and cope with hordes of noisy people watching them day after day.

To make matters worse, few zoos or marine parks make a genuine effort to educate the public, so the real benefits and spin-offs for their wild relatives are very limited. At the end of the day, there is little doubt that most captive animals are there simply to provide cheap entertainment for profit.

Will we ever be able to talk to them?

WHALES, dolphins and porpoises are known to communicate in two main ways: by sound and with body language. They may even be telepathic, as well, and thus able to communicate without speech or movement.

But current evidence suggests that they probably do not have a true language. While they can pass on information such as danger, irritation or sexual interest, they probably cannot complain about the poor size of fish, discuss the vagaries of the weather, or talk about their plans for the future. In other words, they can give simple commands and signals, but probably cannot discuss more abstract concepts.

However, there is no doubt that we still have a great deal to learn about their communication skills. Some dolphins, for example, seem to have their own signature whistles, which are almost the equivalent of human names. They use these to attract the attention of other dolphins and to identify themselves; there is even some evidence to suggest that one dolphin will call the name of another in its group.

In captivity, research has also demonstrated that they can grasp the essential elements of any human language. They do not actually speak, of course, but they can respond correctly to sentences up to five words long. This suggests that they have the potential to develop a language, even if they have not done so in the wild.

Whether or not we will ever be able to communicate with them is another matter altogether. In the past, people predicted that we would be conversing with dolphins, and other small cetaceans, within a few decades; others went so far as to suggest that if an alien intelligence were to attempt to communicate with life on Earth, it might choose dolphins in preference to humans. But these are dreams that have yet to come true.

Bottlenose dolphins with their trainer, The Bahamas

Amazing Facts and Feats
Senses

W HALES, dolphins and porpoises find their way around their underwater world in ways that are well beyond the scope of our own senses.

- **Sight**. The ability to see varies greatly from one species to another. Some of the river dolphins are virtually blind, for example, but most marine cetaceans can see fairly well in both air and water. However, sight is of limited benefit to them since they spend so much of their lives in the dark depths or in turbid water where visibility is poor even close to the surface.

- **Hearing** is far more important. It is effective at night as well as during the day, and does not rely on good visibility. At the same time, sound travels through water nearly five times faster than through air and can be heard over much longer distances. Although cetaceans have lost the distinctive outer ear flaps typical of most other mammals, they do have ears in the form of tiny holes in the skin behind their eyes. Many species can probably also receive sounds through their lower jaws.

- **Taste and smell**. These senses are very similar, because they are both used to detect chemicals. Toothed whales have probably lost their sense of smell altogether, and baleen whales retain only a basic form – mainly because their nostrils (or blowholes) have to remain tightly shut when they dive. Taste is far more important and is used for detecting chemicals both inside and near the outside of the mouth.

- **Touch**. Whales, dolphins and porpoises have very sensitive skin and use their dorsal fins, flippers and beaks to investigate familiar objects, and to touch one another as a form of greeting, or to strengthen social bonds.

- **Geomagnetism** is the least known of all the senses. It involves detecting or 'reading' the Earth's magnetic field, probably using it like an invisible map to navigate over large distances. Many animals, from bacteria and bees to reptiles and birds, are believed to have this sixth sense. But it seems to be particularly well developed in many cetaceans, and may help them to navigate their way across the world's seas and oceans.

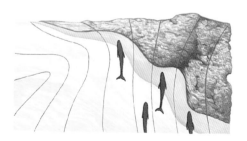

Whales and dolphins may sometimes misread the earth's magnetic field and become stranded

Echolocation: seeing with sound

WHALES, dolphins and porpoises have a remarkable sensory system, called echolocation, which enables them to build up a 'picture' of their underwater surroundings with the help of sound. Bats, shrews, cave swiftlets, oilbirds and a number of other land-based animals use a similar system to hunt fast-moving prey in the dark.

The basic principle of the echolocation system used by cetaceans is quite simple: they transmit ultrasonic clicks into the water, and then monitor and interpret any echoes that bounce back. The clicks are believed to be produced within the nasal plugs, or in the larynx (part of the throat), and are then focused into a directional beam by the fatty melon (which appears as a rounded forehead on most species). The returning echoes may be picked up by the small ear holes on either side of the head, but they are more likely to be transmitted to the brain via the lower jaw.

Bottlenose dolphin using echolocation to find its prey

The system used by many cetaceans is very complex and sophisticated. When homing in on a fish, for example, a dolphin can use echolocation to identify the fish's size and shape, which way it is swimming, its texture, and possibly even its internal structure.

Toothed whales are the real echolocation experts. They use it for keeping track of one another, navigating around objects in the water, identifying changes in sea floor profile, hunting, and monitoring the surroundings for predators or prey. It is even possible that some toothed whales may be able to use particularly powerful blasts of ultrasonic clicks to stun or kill their prey. Baleen whales may also be able to echolocate, but this has never been proven and their system is probably much less well developed.

Short-finned pilot whale, Canary Islands

Record breakers

Largest

The blue whale (below) is the largest animal on Earth. The average adult length is 25 m in males and 26.2 m in females, with body weights of 90–120 tonnes. The heaviest ever recorded was a female which weighed 190 tonnes. The longest ever recorded was another female which measured 33.58 m from the tip of her snout to the end of her tail.

Blue whale, Mexico

Smallest

The black dolphin, Hector's dolphin, finless porpoise and vaquita are probably equal contenders for the title of world's smallest cetacean. All four species can be as short as 1.2 m when fully grown. But in terms of weight, the finless porpoise is probably the lightest, weighing only 30–45 kg.

Humpback whale, New England, USA

Longest flippers
The longest flippers belong to the humpback whale (above). They grow to 23–31 per cent of the length of the whale –a potential maximum of over 5.5 m – but typically measure around 4.6 m in fully grown animals. They are used to herd fish, to manoeuvre while swimming, to comfort their young and to slap the surface of the water.

Tallest dorsal fin
The huge, triangular dorsal fin of the bull killer whale can reach a remarkable height of 1.8 m, which makes it roughly as tall as a man.

Longest baleen plate
The longest baleen is found in the bowhead whale. There are many records within the 3–4 m range, but lengths of up to 5.18 m have been reported for animals killed during the 19th century.

Longest tooth

The male narwhal has two teeth. The one on the right normally remains invisible, but the one on the left grows to a remarkable length. It pierces the animal's upper lip, develops into a long tusk and eventually looks rather like a gnarled and twisted walking stick (left). At least a third of all narwhal tusks are broken, but unbroken tusks reach an average length of about 2 m. In extreme cases, they have been known to exceed 3 m.

Tallest blow

The 'blow' or 'spout' is the cloud of water droplets produced above a whale's head when it blows out. The tallest blow is made by the blue whale: slender and vertical in shape, it reaches an astonishing height of 6–9 m, though blows of up to 12 m have been reported.

Fastest

On 12 October 1958 a bull killer whale was timed swimming at 55.5 km/h in the eastern North Pacific. Similar speeds, albeit in short bursts, have also been reported for Dall's porpoises.

Bull killer whale, or orca, Canada

Largest appetite

A blue whale is believed to eat up to 4 tonnes of krill every day. Since each of these tiny animals weighs only about 1 g, a daily intake of no fewer than 4 million of them is required to keep the whale going. In terms of weight, this is equivalent to eating a fully grown African elephant every day. The whale does not feed all year round, but usually gorges itself for about four months during the summer.

Longest lived

It is difficult to measure the age of a whale accurately, so the maximum life span is not known for most species. However, indirect evidence suggests that some of the larger whales, at least, are able to reach the grand old age of 100 years or more. In 1995, a freshly-killed bowhead whale was being processed in Alaska when the Inuit hunters found

two stone harpoon blades embedded in its blubber.
Since the use of these particular harpoons ended a
century ago, the animal must have been at least 100
years old.

Shortest lived

The harbour porpoise probably has the shortest life
span of any cetacean, with most individuals dying
before they are 8 years old. The oldest harbour
porpoise recorded was believed to be 15 years old.

Longest migration

Humpback whales are inveterate travellers and their
migrations are phenomenal – the longest known of
any mammal. In 1990, for example, one particular
humpback was identified by American biologists off
the Antarctic Peninsula; less then five months later,
it was identified by Colombian biologists off their
own coast, north of the equator. It had travelled
almost 8,700 km. Since then, several other
humpbacks have been identified in both Antarctica
and Colombia, confirming that the first individual
was not simply lost.

Most acrobatic

Many whales, dolphins and porpoises are known for
their aerial displays. Among the larger species,
southern right whales, humpback whales and killer
whales are particularly acrobatic. Humpbacks have
been known to leap almost clear of the water more
than 80 times in a row – which is a phenomenal
achievement considering an average-sized humpback

Humpback whales on migration in Mexico

weighs the equivalent of 400 people.

There are also many outstanding acrobats in the dolphin family. Bottlenose, spotted, striped and dusky dolphins have all been known to hurl themselves as high as 7 m into the air and frequently turn somersaults before re-entering the water. But perhaps the most spectacular acrobat is the long-snouted spinner dolphin, which leaps high into the air, then spins around on its longitudinal axis as many as seven times before splashing back into the water.

CONSERVATION

Endangered species

To the best of our knowledge, no whale, dolphin or porpoise has become extinct in modern times. But a frightening number are in serious trouble, and others have all but disappeared from many of their former haunts. Considering the magnitude of the problems they face, the odds are firmly stacked against them and, for some at least, the future is undoubtedly bleak.

It is difficult to judge which species is the most endangered. Our knowledge is so inadequate that there are no widely accepted population estimates for the vast majority. At the same time, the number of survivors is not the only consideration. The blue whale (below), for example, is not one of the rarest cetaceans in the world but, after decades of intensive whaling, its chances of recovery are severely limited

Blue whale, Mexico

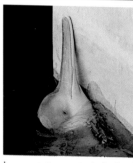

Qi-Qi – the only Yangtze river dolphin in captivity – China

because it is a particularly slow breeder and because its decimated population is widely dispersed.

The Yangtze river dolphin (above) is the rarest cetacean for which population figures are known. There are fewer than 50 individuals (possibly fewer than a couple of dozen), and there is very little chance of rescuing this species. The rarest large whale is the northern right; there are fewer than 320 remaining: despite being officially protected for more than 60 years, its populations have never recovered from hunting. The rarest porpoise is the vaquita or Gulf of California porpoise: its population numbers fewer than 200. Of course, it is possible that some poorly-known species are even rarer than these. For more than a century Longman's beaked whale was known only from two weathered skulls. However, recently there have been more than 40 probable sightings in the western Indian and Pacific oceans. Whether the species is endangered we do not know.

Whaling

COASTAL communities around the world have killed whales for centuries. The blubber and meat provided a welcome source of light, heat and food that were sometimes essential for human survival.

In the old days, this small-scale subsistence hunting probably had only a local impact on whale populations. But by the end of the seventeenth century the character of whaling had changed beyond all recognition. In an age before petroleum or plastics, whales provided valuable raw materials for thousands of everyday products, from soap and candles to whips and corsets. There were huge profits to be made and whaling rapidly became big business.

The slaughter reached its worst excesses around the middle of this century, thanks largely to a series of technological advances in whaling vessels, killing equipment and processing methods. In 1930/31, for example, a record 30,000 blue whales were killed; and, in 1963/64, no fewer than 29,255 sperm whales were killed.

One by one, without pity, the great whales were hunted almost to the point of extinction. In the space of a few hundred years, literally millions of them were killed around the world. Today, we are left merely with the tattered remains: in most cases, no more than 5–10 per cent of their original populations. The North Atlantic grey whale is extinct; there are fewer than 320 surviving northern right whales; the bowhead has all but disappeared from vast areas of its former range; and so the catalogue of destruction unfolds.

Yet, incredibly, we still have not learnt the lessons of the past. The story of commercial whaling continues as Norway and Japan persist in hunting whales in the North Atlantic, the North Pacific and the Antarctic. In blatant defiance of world opinion, they are gradually expanding their activities and, alarmingly, they are being watched with considerable interest by other nations that may decide to resume whaling themselves.

To make matters even worse, it is virtually impossible to kill whales humanely. In some cases, it can take as long as an hour for them to die agonising

Traditional whaling vessel, The Azores

deaths after explosive harpoons have blown huge, gaping holes in their bodies. As one ex-whaler commented: 'if whales could scream, whaling would have stopped many years ago'.

Whale bones, Antarctic Peninsula

Hunting small cetaceans

LARGE whales are not the only cetaceans to suffer from hunting. It is believed that hundreds of thousands of small whales, dolphins and porpoises are killed every year in seas and oceans around the world. Nets, knives, rifles, hand-held harpoons and even explosive harpoons are used for the killing.

One of the most controversial of these hunts takes place in the Faroes, a group of islands lying

Discarded remains of a dusky dolphin, Peru

halfway between Scotland and Iceland, in the north-east Atlantic. Entire pods of long-finned pilot whales are herded into sandy bays by men in small boats, during noisy 'drives' that frequently take many hours to complete. All the animals – including pregnant and nursing females and their babies – are dragged ashore with steel hooks, called gaffs, and then killed with long knives. In the last 300 years, more than a quarter of a million long-finned pilot whales have been killed in approximately 1,700 different drives. An average of around 1,200 whales have been taken each year during the past decade.

The Faroese defend the hunt vigorously, arguing that it is a traditional part of their culture and provides a free and welcome source of protein. But opponents to the hunt argue that it is terribly cruel and no longer necessary in such a modern society with a relatively high standard of living; they also argue that no-one knows enough about the number of pilot whales around the Faroes, their wider distribution and movements throughout the year, or any of the other dangers they face, to judge whether or not the hunt is a threat to their future survival.

Equipment used for hunting pilot whales in the Faroes

Conflicts with fisheries

S INCE the 1950s, the staggering growth of many modern fisheries and the introduction of increasingly destructive fishing methods have spelt disaster for whales, dolphins and porpoises around the world.

Hundreds of thousands of them – possibly even millions – die slow, lingering deaths in fishing nets every year. Many more could be threatened by the sheer scale of modern fisheries, which over-exploit fish stocks with scant regard for the future health of the world's oceans.

Drift-netting is one of the worst culprits and, indeed, is probably the most indiscriminate method of fishing ever devised. Hanging in the water, unseen and undetectable, drift nets are carried freely with the ocean currents and winds. Dubbed 'walls of death', or 'curtains of death', they catch everything in their path, from seabirds and turtles to whales and dolphins. Each net can be as long as 50 km and, although lengths of over 2.5 km are now illegal in many parts of the world, there are more than enough of them floating around the world's seas and oceans at any one time to circle the Earth at the equator.

Gill nets are similar to drift nets in design, although much smaller, and pose another serious threat. Since they are relatively inexpensive, these deathtraps are used along coastlines and in major rivers worldwide, from New Zealand and Sri Lanka to Canada and Britain. Tens of thousands of small cetaceans are believed to drown in them every year.

But perhaps the most infamous culprit, responsible for killing more dolphins in the past 35 years than any other human activity, is the tuna-fishing industry. In the eastern tropical Pacific, a stretch of ocean extending from southern California to Chile and covering an area roughly the size of Canada, it has directly caused the deaths of an estimated 6–12 million dolphins. In the worst period, during the 1960s and early 1970s, as many as half a million dolphins were being killed in the region *every year*. Fortunately, public outrage has forced the authorities to introduce new rules and regulations, and the scale of the slaughter has dropped to about 4,000 deaths a year. It is still too many, and there is mounting evidence to suggest that dolphins are being set on by tuna-fishing fleets in other parts of the world, but progress is slowly being made.

Unfortunately, there are no easy solutions to

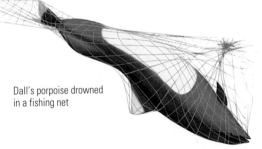

Dall's porpoise drowned
in a fishing net

most conflicts with fisheries. In some cases, a simple modification of the nets or the fishery management systems can have a positive effect. Educational programmes for fishermen, and newly-developed devices which alert whales and dolphins to the presence of nets, may also work in some situations. But there is no escaping the fact that much more drastic action, such as seasonal closures of some

Long-snouted spinner dolphin for sale in fish market, Sri Lanka

Pollution

SOME experts predict that pollution could be the most serious threat to whales, dolphins and porpoises in the future. It is a silent, insidious and widespread killer that is already causing severe problems around the world.

Despite all the warnings, many governments continue to pretend that the world's seas and oceans have an infinite capacity to absorb the waste products of human activities. Ever-increasing quantities of industrial waste, agricultural chemicals, radioactive discharges, untreated sewage, oil, modern plastic debris and a wide variety of other pollutants are dumped directly into the sea every day – or slowly make their way there via rivers – often with devastating effect.

We are only just beginning to learn about the precise details of the damage they cause. Some pollutants are so toxic, or are present in such huge quantities, that they cause immediate death. Others are more subtle in their effects, but nonetheless may be responsible for weeks, months or even years of prolonged suffering.

Unfortunately, whales, dolphins, porpoises and other top predators are particularly vulnerable to pollution. This is because the toxins are passed along the food chain: minute quantities are picked up by marine plankton, which are then eaten by fish and squid, and these in turn are eaten by the predators themselves. The further along the chain, the higher the concentration of toxins. Worse still, much of this build-up is passed on from one generation to another: a lactating female, through her milk, can deliver the toxins in highly concentrated doses to her young calf.

Underwater noise pollution is also very worrying. Caused by a variety of human activities, from coastal development and seismic testing to speed boats and heavy shipping, it is a particular problem for whales, dolphins and porpoises, which rely on sound for many of their day-to-day activities. Unfortunately, it is not only the loudness of a noise that is important, but its frequency as well – some frequencies are likely to be more disturbing than others, depending on the hearing range of different species.

Rubbish on a beach in the Black Sea, Georgia

Habitat degradation

LIKE wildlife on land, whales, dolphins and
porpoises also suffer from habitat degradation,
and disturbance, although in different ways.

The main problem areas are rivers, close to the
shore, and near human activities further out to sea.
Coastal and riverbank development, land
reclamation, deep-sea dumping, oil, gas and mineral
exploration, commercial fish farming, boat traffic,
and the effects of land-based activities such as
deforestation and river damming are all to blame.

Their consequences can be quite subtle, such as
increased amounts of sediment or changes in
salinity, but they can also be extremely dramatic.
Habitat degradation along the coast, for example,
can have a far-reaching impact on the marine
environment as a whole, since this is where nurseries
for all kinds of animals form the foundation of the
sea's complex food webs.

River dolphins are probably the hardest-hit. The
threats their habitats face include heavy boat traffic,
riverbank development and dam construction. In the
case of the highly endangered Yangtze river dolphin,
for example, the world's largest hydroelectric project
at the famous Three Gorges, in Hubei Province, is
likely to be the final nail in its coffin.

To make matters worse, many of the species and
populations most affected by habitat degradation
already have restricted distributions, or their
requirements tie them to coasts or rivers and prevent

Bathers on a crowded beach in Peru

them from 'escaping' to safer areas. These include all the river dolphins, the vaquita, Burmeister's porpoise, Hector's dolphin, and several large whales that move inshore at certain times of the year to breed.

One solution to the problem is to provide the animals with special sanctuaries, or marine reserves, in which they can feed and breed in relative safety. Some already exist, such as the ones in the Southern and Indian Oceans, but they need better legislation to be truly effective. Meanwhile, of course, many more protected areas are needed.

40. False killer whale (*Pseudorca crassidens*) (p. 121)
Other names: false pilot whale, pseudorca
41. Long-finned pilot whale (*Globicephala melas*) (p. 122)
Other names: caaing whale, longfin pilot whale, Atlantic pilot whale, blackfish, pothead whale
42. Short-finned pilot whales (*Globicephala macrorhynchus*) (p. 122)
Other names: shortfin pilot whale, Pacific pilot whale, blackfish, pothead whale
43. Killer whale (*Orcinus orca*) (p. 124)
Other names: orca, blackfish, great killer whale
44. Tucuxi (*Sotalia fluviatilis*) (p. 126)
Other names: estuarine dolphin
45. Long-snouted spinner dolphin (*Stenella longirostris*) (p. 127)
Other names: spinner, longsnout, rollover, long-beaked dolphin
46. Short-snouted spinner dolphin (*Stenella clymene*) (p. 128)
Other names: Clymene dolphin, Senegal dolphin, Helmet dolphin
47. Striped dolphin (*Stenella coeruleoalba*) (p. 129)
Other names: streaker porpoise, euphrosyne dolphin, whitebelly, Meyen's dolphin, blue-white dolphin, Gray's dolphin
48. Pantropical spotted dolphin (*Stenella attenuata*) (p. 130)
Other names: spotted dolphin, spotter, spotted porpoise, white-spotted dolphin, slender-beaked dolphin
49. Atlantic spotted dolphin (*Stenella frontalis*) (p. 131)
Other names: spotted porpoise, long-snouted dolphin, spotter, bridled dolphin, Gulf Stream spotted dolphin
50. Atlantic hump-backed dolphin (*Sousa teuszii*) (p. 132)
Other names: Atlantic humpback dolphin, Cameroon dolphin
51. Indo-Pacific hump-backed dolphin (*Sousa chinensis*) (p. 133)
Other names: Indo-Pacific humpback dolphin, speckled dolphin, Chinese white dolphin, pink dolphin
52. Northern rightwhale dolphin (*Lissodelphis borealis*) (p. 134)
Other names: Pacific rightwhale porpoise
53. Southern rightwhale dolphin (*Lissodelphis peronii*) (p. 135)
Other names: mealy-mouthed porpoise
54. Long-beaked common dolphin (*Delphinus capensis*) (p. 136)
Other names: criss-cross dolphin, saddleback dolphin, cape dolphin, white-bellied porpoise, common porpoise

55. Short-beaked common dolphin (*Delphinus delphis*) (p. 136)
Other names: criss-cross dolphin, saddleback dolphin, cape dolphin, white-bellied porpoise, common porpoise

56. Rough-toothed dolphin (*Steno bredanensis*) (p. 138)
Other names: slopehead

57. Risso's dolphin (*Grampus griseus*) (p. 139)
Other names: grey dolphin, grey grampus, grampus, white-head grampus

58. Irrawaddy dolphin (*Orcaella brevirostris*) (p. 140)
Other names: snubfin dolphin

59. Fraser's dolphin (*Lagenodelphis hosei*) (p. 141)
Other names: Fraser's porpoise, white-bellied dolphin, Sarawak dolphin, shortsnout dolphin, Bornean dolphin

60. Bottlenose dolphin (*Tursiops truncatus*) (p. 142)
Other names: bottle-nosed dolphin, Atlantic (or Pacific) bottlenose dolphin, cowfish, grey porpoise, black porpoise

61. Commerson's dolphin (*Cephalorhynchus commersonii*) (p. 144)
Other names: skunk dolphin, jacobite, puffing pig, piebald dolphin, black and white dolphin

62. Hector's dolphin (*Cephalorhynchus hectori*) (p. 145)
Other names: New Zealand dolphin, New Zealand white-front dolphin, little pied dolphin

63. Heaviside's dolphin (*Cephalorhynchus heavisidii*) (p. 146)
Other names: Benguela dolphin, South African dolphin

64. Black dolphin (*Cephalorhynchus eutropia*) (p. 147)
Other names: white-bellied dolphin, Chilean black dolphin, Chilean dolphin

65. Hourglass dolphin (*Lagenorhynchus cruciger*) (p. 148)
Other names: southern white-sided dolphin, Wilson's dolphin

66. Peale's dolphin (*Lagenorhynchus australis*) (p. 149)
Other names: southern dolphin, Peale's porpoise, blackchin dolphin, black-chinned dolphin

67. Atlantic white-sided dolphin (*Lagenorhynchus acutus*) (p. 150)
Other names: lag, jumper, springer, Atlantic white-sided porpoise

68. Pacific white-sided dolphin (*Lagenorhynchus obliquidens*) (p. 151)
Other names: lag, white-striped dolphin, Pacific striped dolphin, hook-finned porpoise

69. Dusky dolphin (*Lagenorhynchus obscurus*) (p. 152)
Other names: Fitzroy's dolphin
70. White-beaked dolphin (*Lagenorhynchus albirostris*) (p. 153)
Other names: white-beaked porpoise, white-nosed dolphin, squidhound

FAMILY: PONTOPORIIDAE
71. Yangtze river dolphin (*Lipotes vexillifer*) (p. 154)
Other names: baiji, beiji, pei c'hi, whitefin dolphin, whiteflag dolphin, Chinese river dolphin
72. Franciscana (*Pontoporia blainvillei*) (p. 156)
Other names: La Plata dolphin

FAMILY: PLATANISTIDAE
73. Ganges river dolphin (*Platanista gangetica*) (p. 159)
Other names: Ganges susu, blind river dolphin, side-swimming dolphin, Gangetic dolphin
74. Indus river dolphin (*Platanista minor*) (p. 158)
Other names: Indus susu, blind river dolphin, side-swimming dolphin, bhulan

FAMILY: INIIDAE
75. Amazon river dolphin (*Inia geoffrensis*) (p. 157)
Other names: boto, pink porpoise, pink dolphin

FAMILY: PHOCOENIDAE
76. Vaquita (*Phocoena sinus*) (p. 160)
Other names: Gulf of California porpoise, cochito
77. Harbour porpoise (*Phocoena phocoena*) (p. 161)
Other names: common porpoise, puffing pig
78. Burmeister's porpoise (*Phocoena spinipinnis*) (p. 162)
Other names: black porpoise
79. Finless porpoise (*Neophocaena phocaenoides*) (p. 163)
Other names: black porpoise, black finless porpoise, jiangzhu
80. Spectacled porpoise (*Australophocaena dioptrica*) (p. 164)
Formerly known as *Phocoena dioptrica*
81. Dall's porpoise (*Phocoenoides dalli*) (p. 165)
Other names: spray porpoise, white-flanked porpoise, True's porpoise

Glossary

Amphipod Small, shrimp-like crustacean that is a food source for some whales.

Antarctic Convergence Natural boundary of the Southern Ocean, where cold waters from the south sink below warmer waters from the north; lying roughly between 50°–60°S, it shifts slightly with the seasons.

Baleen/baleen plates Comb-like plates hanging down from the upper jaws of many large whales; used instead of teeth to capture prey.

Baleen whale Sub-order of whales with baleen plates instead of teeth, known in the scientific world as Mysticeti.

Beak Elongated snout of many cetaceans.

Blow Cloud of water vapour exhaled by cetaceans (also known as the 'spout'); often used to describe the act of breathing.

Blowhole(s) Nasal opening(s) or nostril(s) on the top of the head.

Blubber Layer of fat just beneath the skin of marine mammals; important for insulation instead of fur.

Bow-riding Riding in the pressure wave in front of a boat, ship or large whale.

Breaching Leaping completely (or nearly completely) out of the water, and landing back with a splash.

Bubble-netting Feeding technique used by humpback whales in which they produce fishing nets by blowing bubbles underwater.

Callosity Area of roughened skin on the head of a right whale, to which whale lice and barnacles attach.

Cetacean Any member of the order Cetacea, which includes all whales, dolphins and porpoises.

Copepod A small crustacean that is a food source for some whales.

Crustacean Member of a class of invertebrates (animals without backbones) that are food for many marine animals; mostly aquatic.

Dorsal fin Raised structure on the back of most (but not all) cetaceans; not supported by bone.

Drift-net Fishing net which hangs in the water, unseen and undetectable, and is carried freely with the ocean currents and winds; strongly criticised for catching everything in its path, from seabirds and turtles to whales and dolphins.

Echolocation Process of sending out sounds and interpreting the returning echoes to build up a 'sound picture', as in sonar; used by many cetaceans to orientate, navigate and find food.

Flipper Flattened, paddle-shaped limb of a marine mammal; refers to the front limb of a cetacean (also known as the 'pectoral fin').

Flipper-slapping Raising a flipper out of the water and slapping it onto the surface.

Fluke Horizontally flattened tail of a cetacean; contains no bone.

Fluking Raising the tail flukes into the air upon diving.

Gill net Similar to a drift net in design, although much smaller and fixed in one position near the coast or in a river.

Hydrophone Waterproofed, underwater microphone.

Keel Distinctive bulge on the tail stock near the flukes.

Krill Small, shrimp-like crustaceans that form the major food of many large whales; there are about 80 different species, ranging from 8–60 mm in length.

Lobtailing Slapping tail flukes against the water, creating a splash.

Logging Lying still at or near the water surface.

Mandible Lower jaw of the skull.

Melon Fatty organ in the bulging forehead of many toothed cetaceans, believed to be used to focus sounds for echolocation.

Pectoral fin See 'flipper'.

Photo-identification Technique for studying cetaceans using photographs as a permanent record of identifiable individuals.

Pod Coordinated group of whales; term normally used for larger, toothed whales.

Polar Region around either the South Pole or North Pole.

Porpoising Leaping out of the water while swimming at speed.

Purse-seine net Long net set around a shoal of fish, then gathered at the bottom and drawn in to form a 'purse'.

Rorqual Baleen whale of the genus *Balaenoptera*; many experts also include the humpback whale (genus *Megaptera*) in this group.

Rostrum Upper jaw of the skull (may be used to refer to the beak or snout).

School Coordinated group of cetaceans; term normally used in association with dolphins.

Snout See 'beak'.

Sonar See 'echolocation'.

Spout See 'blow'.

Spyhopping Raising the head vertically out of the water, apparently to look around above the surface.

Submarine canyon Deep, steep-sided valley in the continental shelf.

Tail stock Muscular region of the tail between the flukes and the dorsal fin.

Temperate Mid-latitude regions of the world between the tropics and the poles.

Toothed whale Sub-order of whales with teeth, known in the scientific world as Odontoceti.

Tropical Low-latitude regions of the world between the tropics of Capricorn and Cancer.

Tubercles Circular bumps found on some cetaceans; usually along the edges of flippers and dorsal fins, but also on a humpback whale's head.

Turbid Muddy or cloudy water carrying lots of sediment.

Wake-riding Swimming in the frothy wake of a boat or ship.

Whalebone Another name for baleen.

Index

COLLINS GEM
BABIES'
names
a ? z
'a mine of information'

COLLINS GEM
BEER
'a mine of information'

COLLINS GEM
BIRDS
'a mine of information'

COLLINS GEM
CALORIE
Counter
'a mine of information'

COLLINS GEM
FACT FILE
?
'a mine of information'

COLLINS GEM
FENG SHUI
'a mine of information'

COLLINS GEM
FLAGS
'a mine of information'

COLLINS GEM
Healthy
EATING
'a mine of information'

COLLINS GEM
QUOTATIONS
"
'a mine of information'

COLLINS GEM
SAS
Self-Defence
'a mine of information'

COLLINS GEM
SAS
Survival Guide
'a mine of information'

COLLINS GEM
SEASHORE
'a mine of information'

COLLINS GEM
TREES
'a mine of information'

COLLINS GEM
Understanding
DREAMS
'a mine of information'

COLLINS GEM
WILD
flowers
'a mine of information'

COLLINS GEM
WINE
Dictionary
'a mine of information'